I'M A MICHIGANDER

Written by Russell Slater
Illustrated by Jordan Richardson

ISBN-13: 978-0692375709

ISBN-10: 0692375708

Peninsulam Publishing

Publishing stories Made in Michigan

www.peninsulampublishing.com

Printed in the USA

"Special thanks to my wife, Marissa, for your help and support.
For Eli – and all little Michiganders. If you seek a pleasant peninsula, look around you." -R.S.

"Dedicated to Jet and Jorgia, and to my wife, Jessica, for always encouraging me." –J.R.

This Book Belongs to

_____

I'm a Michigander,
and it fills me with delight!

I love this BIG ole state,
it's really quite a sight!

Cities and farms...
towns from BIG to small...

We have a little bit of everything,
Michigan has it all.

I'm a Michigander, I love to play outside.

Here in Michigan, There's always room to hide!

Lakes of every shape and size,
some so big and deep

Folks still call them "GREAT,"
treasures we shall keep.

I'm a Michigander,
and I wish I were a king!

I guess that means I'd have to
move to our capital, Lansing.

Whether Tulip Time in Holland,
or swimming our Great Lakes

We're sure to have GREAT fun,
whatever it may take.

I'm a Michigander,
I love to have a ball!

WELCOME TO

GRAND HAVEN

COAST GUARD CITY USA

I like to watch the boats float by
at the Coast Guard Festival.

Up in Traverse City, they have cherries Galore!

Traverse City

You may even find them at your local grocery store.

Hold up your hand, what do you see?
Your hand looks like Michigan,

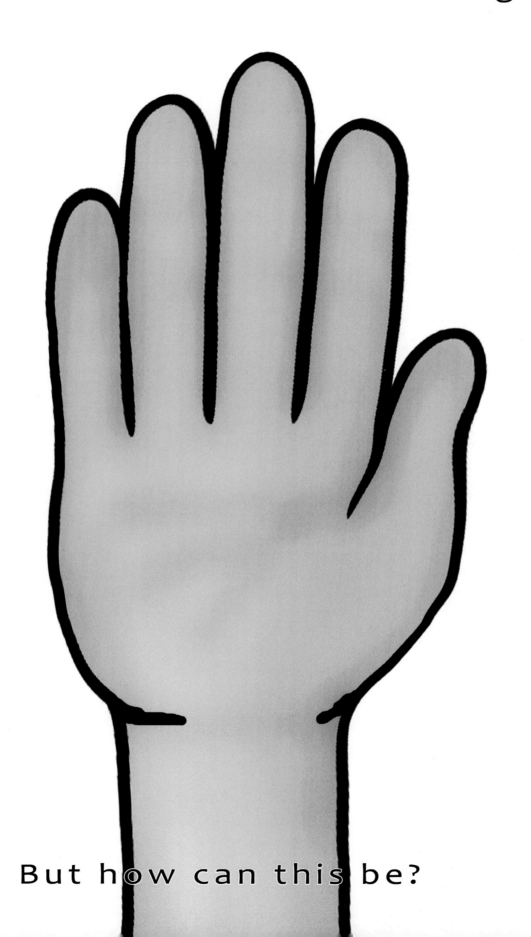

But how can this be?

Because Michigan is the Mitten State,
We give directions on our hand.

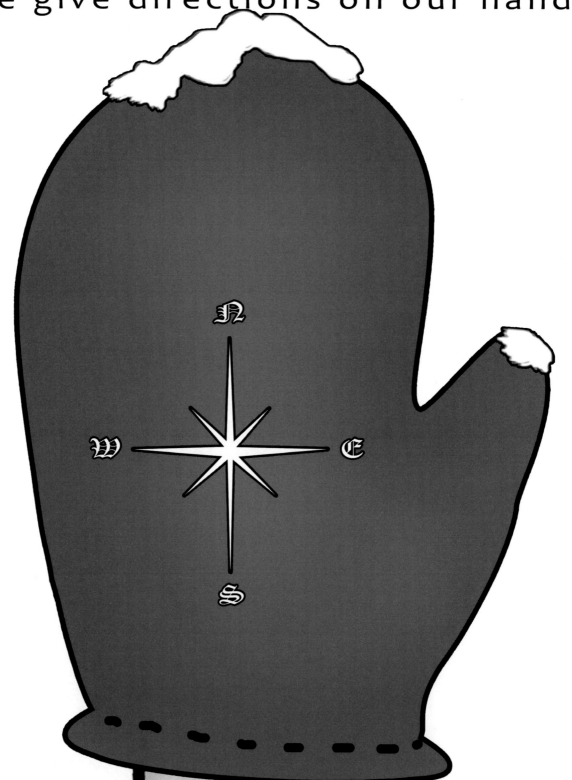

We like to help each other,
throughout this beautiful land.

I'm a Michigander,
I love to learn in school

Ann Arbor is home to one
that I've heard is pretty cool!

I'm a Michigander,
And this is what I know...

Sometimes in the winter,
We get buried by the SNOW!

I'm a Michigander, I like what I see

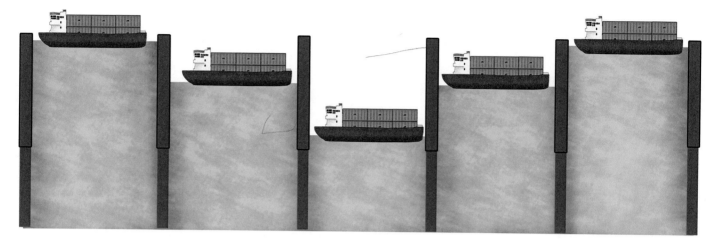

When I visit the Soo Locks up in Sault Ste. Marie.

CANADA

MICHIGAN

Marquette may seem far away,
With its Lake Superior beach

But like all of
Michigan,
it's really quite
easy to reach.

You can ride a
horse drawn carriage,
or get fudge by the pound.

It's the cutest little island,
the best I ever found.

I'm a Michigander,
I love to walk for miles.

NILES

I could walk to Indiana, but I
think I'll stop at Niles.

Leaving Michigan for Wisconsin?
Surely a mistake!

Hurry back,
Take the S.S. Badger across the lake.

I'm a Michigander,
I have been from the start.

No matter where I go,
the state is in my heart.

Let the good times begin,
wherever we may be.

I ♥ MI

I love my dear ole Michigan,
as you can plainly see.

I'm a Michigander and proud to call it home.

When I think of Michigan,
I know I'm not alone.

I'm a Michigander,
it's what I'll always be.

Michigan is forever home.

Home sweet home to me.

20654769R00019